NO MORE ~~MIND GAMES~~

ALSO BY JOSEPH PRINCE

For more information on these books and
other inspiring resources, visit JosephPrince.com.

JOSEPH PRINCE

No More Mind Games

WIN OVER DISCOURAGEMENT AND DEPRESSION

Cover design by 22 Media Pte Ltd.
Cover copyright © 2018 by 22 Media Pte Ltd.

All Scripture quotations, unless otherwise indicated, are taken from the New King James Version. Copyright © 1982 by Thomas Nelson, Inc. Used by permission. All rights reserved.

Scripture quotations marked KJV are taken from the King James Version of the Bible.

Scripture quotations marked NLT are taken from the Holy Bible, New Living Translation. Copyright ©1996, 2004, 2007, 2013 by Tyndale House Foundation. Used by permission of Tyndale House Publishers, Inc., Carol Stream, Illinois 60188. All rights reserved.

Scripture quotations marked AMP are taken from the Amplified® Bible. Copyright © 2015 by The Lockman Foundation. Used by permission. (www.lockman.org)

Scripture quotations marked NIV are taken from the Holy Bible, New International Version, NIV. Copyright © 1973, 1978, 1984, 2011 by Biblica, Inc. Used by permission of Zondervan. All rights reserved worldwide. (www.zondervan.com)

No More Mind Games: Win over Discouragement and Depression

ISBN 978-981-11-8134-4

© Copyright Joseph Prince, 2018
Joseph Prince Resources
www.JosephPrince.com

Printed in the Republic of Singapore
First edition, first print: September 2018

CONTENTS

INTRODUCTION

If you are going through a season of severe discouragement, and find yourself battling depression and suicidal thoughts, I believe the Lord has a word for you today. Don't give in to the darkness that is threatening to overwhelm you. Don't believe the LIE that you have been an utter failure and that there is only one way to end the misery and pain that have weighed you down for so long. You are *not* alone. You may not feel it right now, but I want you to know that God loves you and has a plan for your life. It is not by accident that you are holding this book in your hands. He has somehow orchestrated it, and I pray that you will read on and give me a chance to share God's heart for you.

There is an enemy who wants to isolate you. He is playing mind games with you and wants to make you feel like you are a failure and that there is no hope. He wants to steal your peace, your joy, and every good thing in your life. This enemy wants to destroy and kill you. BUT there is also a God who cares for you so intimately, a God who sees the pain you are going through, and who paid the price for you to enjoy, not simply *endure*, this life. Our Lord Jesus said, "The thief does not come except to steal, and to kill, and to destroy. I have come that they may have life, and that they may have *it* more abundantly" (John 10:10). My friend, this is God's desire for you: He wants you to have a rich and satisfying life, and to enjoy life to the fullest.

I do not know what burdens you carry. Perhaps you are struggling with a secret addiction, and shame has stripped you bare. Perhaps you have been confronted with failure after failure, and it is building up to a point where you can see no way out. Perhaps you have been told over and over again that you are worthless, and demeaning things have been said and done to you. Maybe you have been struggling with various issues for so long, you are at a point where you are numb, just exhausted, and you are ready to give up. Maybe things look great on your Instagram highlight reel, but on the inside, you feel a growing emptiness, a sense of being trapped, and that things will never get better.

I do not claim to have the answers to the questions that are weighing you down. I can't tell you why your husband betrayed you, or why your company retrenched you just like that. I can't explain why the medications you have been taking don't seem to work, or why you can't seem to stop the sadness that is eating you up.

What I can tell you is that the Bible is not silent on the sufferings you are going through. May the accounts that I will be sharing with you open your eyes to who God is, and how deeply He loves *you*. I pray that as you allow me to take this journey with you, the Lord will show you truths that will cause your heart to be filled with a supernatural peace that surpasses understanding, truths that will break you free from the bondages of depression. You may feel like giving up on yourself, but God is not willing to let you do that.

Would you allow me to introduce you to a God who wants to take your brokenness and despair, and give you His joy in exchange? Would you allow me to tell you about a God who comes to you in your darkest moments, a God who has given up everything so that you never ever need to feel alone? And would you allow me to show you some practical steps you can take as you put your hand in His, and let Him love you back into wholeness?

Thank you so much. I am praying with you for your breakthrough, and I believe your best days are ahead of you.

CHAPTER 1

You Are Not Alone

1

YOU ARE *Not Alone*

I believe we are living in a time when the enemy is increasingly using the weapons of discouragement and depression, and I feel an urgency to proclaim the truth of God's Word in this area. I see this in society at large, where several high-profile suicides by prominent celebrities over the past few years have shocked and saddened people around the world. I see it in the mounting rates of opioid dependency, depression, anxiety, and loneliness, together with increasing incidents of suicide.[1] But I also see it in the body of Christ, where more than ever before, the enemy seems to be using discouragement and depression to come against pastors, leaders, and other precious individuals who have been pouring their hearts out for the people of God.

My team and I have also received many prayer requests

from people grappling with depression and anxiety. Some of them are suffering from post-traumatic stress disorder. Some of them are grappling with postnatal depression. Some appear to have it all together but feel like they are trapped and that their lives have no meaning. Many of them feel mentally and emotionally exhausted. They are often overwhelmed and discouraged by the multiple situations they face, and feel alone in their struggles. Many cannot see any hope in their lives and are on the brink of giving up.

If you are reading this, and what I have described sounds painfully familiar to you, I want you to know it is not by coincidence you are reading the words on this page. I really believe you are reading these words because you have cried out to the Lord for help, and this is Him answering you. Or maybe you don't know God, but you have friends and loved ones who do. If so, you may be holding one of the ways the Lord is answering their prayers for you, and my prayer is that you will come to know the Lord by the time you reach the end of this book.

Whatever circumstances you might be facing, and whatever brought this book into your hands, I pray that as you read on, your eyes will be opened to see the length, the breadth, the depth, and the height of His exceeding love for you. I pray that you will have a revelation of our Lord Jesus that will expose and shatter every lie the enemy has used to imprison you, break the bondage of depression in your life, and cause hope to spring forth in your heart. I pray that you will be set free from every oppressive thought, every addiction, every brokenness, and every sense of hopelessness, failure, and rejection as you begin to see more and more of our Lord Jesus, who is your "very present help" in the midst of your trouble (Ps. 46:1)!

They Were Discouraged Too

I want to start by showing you that depression, anxiety, and despair are not modern conditions. Throughout the Bible, we find men and women who had cried out to God in the midst of their discouragement, with some of them expressing suicidal thoughts. Here are just a few examples of Bible characters who had gone through bouts of depression. I pray that their stories will help you to catch a revelation of the Lord's heart for you.

First Kings 19 tells us about how Elijah, a mighty

prophet who had called down fire from heaven and raised the dead, came to a point in his life where, hounded by his enemies, he got so discouraged that he prayed he might die. The Bible records how he cried out to God, "Now, LORD, take my life, for I *am* no better than my fathers!" (1 Kings 19:4).

God had worked powerful miracles through Elijah's hands, but when Elijah *saw* that his enemies wanted to kill him, he forgot the God who had led him to Cherith and brought ravens to feed him by day and evening. He forgot about the barrel of meal that never ran out and the jar of oil that never ran dry. He forgot the God of the resurrection who raised the widow's son back to life, the God who answers by fire, the God who could hold back and send the rain (see 1 Kings 17; 18:24, 38–45). This tells us that even if we have seen God do great things in our lives, it is so easy for us to be like Elijah when we get snared by visible things that are temporal, and lose sight of the invisible God who is eternal.

In the Gospels, we find the story of the Gadarene demoniac who lived among the tombs. In Mark's account, we read how "always, night and day," he was "crying out and cutting himself with stones" (Mark 5:5).

Luke 24 shares the account of two disciples who were on the road to Emmaus. They had pinned their hopes on Jesus being the promised Messiah who would rescue Israel, but then He was taken by soldiers and crucified, and now they were "brokenhearted" (Luke 24:17 AMP).

Perhaps you are no stranger to the despair and anguish captured in these stories. Perhaps like Elijah, you feel like an utter failure in your ministry or career. You are completely disappointed with yourself, and you feel like you do not deserve to live anymore. Perhaps you feel like your best days are behind you and now, you are just a burden to others. Or perhaps you have been under tremendous stress at work or in your family, and you are just so tired of fighting one battle only to be faced with another.

You are not alone. You have a *good God* who loves you.

Maybe like the man in Gadara, you have been tormented by the demons of your past. Perhaps, like him, you have been isolating yourself, and the thoughts that fill your mind are morbid and full of death. Perhaps something happened to you, and you have been cutting yourself to express the deep self-loathing and hurt you cannot put into words, inflicting physical pain on yourself in the hope that it would drown the mental and emotional pain inside you. Or perhaps like the two disciples, you had pinned your hopes on something or someone, and now your heart is broken because your hopes have been crushed. It could be family members who seem to have abandoned you, leaving you feeling alone, helpless, and afraid. Whatever you are going through, the enemy wants you to think no one understands. Today, I pray that you will see that *you are not alone.* You have a good God who loves you and whose faithfulness endures to all generations (see Ps. 119:90)!

God Has Not Abandoned You

The Bible tells us Elijah was alone in the wilderness when he cried out to God. The angel of the Lord came to him as he slept and woke him up to eat some fresh bread baked over hot coals, and to drink from a jar of water (see 1 Kings 19:5–6 niv). Elijah ate and drank, and then he laid down again. And the angel of the Lord came back a second time and touched him, and said, "Arise *and* eat, because the journey *is* too great for you" (1 Kings 19:7).

When you find "the angel of the Lord" in the Old Testament, in most instances it refers to the pre-incarnate appearance of Christ. What a beautiful picture of our Lord Jesus seeking us out to strengthen and feed us during our seasons of discouragement! In the day of Elijah's faith, ravens fed him and a widow sustained him (see 1 Kings 17:3–6, 8–15). But in the day of his depression, angels waited on him, and God Himself came to him and fed him.

The same Jesus who looked for Elijah in the wilderness also sought out the Gadarene demoniac among the forsaken tombs. The Gospel of Mark records how our Lord Jesus had spent a whole day teaching the multitudes but when evening came, He instructed His disciples to bring Him over to the country of the Gadarenes on the other side of the Sea of Galilee. I believe He had heard the cry of one man and traveled across the Sea of Galilee for one reason—to deliver that man. The man "had demons for a long time" (Luke 8:27), but after just one encounter with Jesus, he was freed from his oppression. Later, he was found "sitting at the feet of Jesus, clothed and in his right mind" (Luke 8:35). It doesn't matter how long you have been bound by depressive thoughts that grip your mind. In one instance, our Lord Jesus can set you free. That is my prayer for you today.

As for the two disciples, the Bible tells us that as they conversed on the road to Emmaus, "**Jesus Himself** drew near and went with them" (Luke 24:15, boldface mine). And He said to them, "What kind of conversation *is* this that you have with one another as you walk and are sad?" (Luke 24:17). Do you know that our Lord Jesus notices it when you are sad? The people around you may not know what you are going through—they see only the happy pictures you post on social media and know nothing of the emptiness and despair you have learned to hide so well— but Jesus knows. He knows your secret sadness, and He Himself is drawing near to you.

Do you want to know what our Lord Jesus did to lift the two disciples out of their despondency? The Bible tells us that "He expounded to them in all the Scriptures the things concerning Himself" (Luke 24:27). The more we see Jesus in the Scriptures, the more sadness loses its hold on us. The disciples later said to each other, "Did not our heart burn within us while He talked with us on the road, and while He opened the Scriptures to us?" (Luke 24:32).

If you feel your heart burning within you now, that's your Lord Jesus speaking to you and revealing His love to you. But even if you do not feel anything, I know He is reaching out to you even as I write these words. He loves you—more than you can ever comprehend!

You Are Not Alone

Maybe you have believed the lie that you are alone in your discouragement and depression. I pray that you have caught a glimpse of a God who loves you, a God who knows you are hurting. He is seeking you out right now. He is not waiting for you to get your act together. Our Lord Jesus is not far away and indifferent to your pain. His heart is filled with love and compassion toward you. His name in Hebrew is *Yeshua* and it means "salvation."[2] Today, He wants to save you.

He knows how heavy your burdens are and how exhausted you feel. He knows the journey ahead is too great for you. Right now, He is saying to you, "Come to Me, all *you* who labor and are heavy laden, and I will give you rest" (Matt. 11:28). If you are weary, and the burden you are carrying has grown too heavy for you, you are eligible for His invitation. Will you take it up, and let Him carry you? Will you give Him your burdens and receive His rest?

Jesus prepared bread for Elijah and fed him when he had no more will to live. But do you know that He also prepared bread for His disciples when they were worn out from fishing all night and had caught nothing?

Maybe you know what it feels like to toil all night and catch absolutely nothing. Maybe you have been trying again and again to get out of that addiction, but all your efforts have come to naught. The Gospel of John records how the disciples returned to the shore and saw "a fire of coals there, and fish laid on it, and bread" (John 21:9). Jesus declared, "I am the bread of life. Whoever comes to me will never go hungry, and whoever believes in me will never be thirsty" (John 6:35 NIV).

He is preparing bread for *you* right now, and He is inviting you to partake of Him. Has it been a long night for you? He is saying to you, "Come *and* eat breakfast" (John 21:12).

In and of your own strength, you cannot get yourself out of your depression. Your willpower is not enough to force yourself out of the darkness and despair. But when you partake of our Lord Jesus and His finished work on the cross, you can receive supernatural strength.

After Elijah ate, the Bible records that he was strengthened by the food, and he traveled for forty days and forty nights (see 1 Kings 19:8). Jesus' body was broken for you that you might be whole—spirit, soul, and body. Partake of Him today by meditating on all He has done for you on the cross. Allow Him to strengthen and sustain you. And as you put your trust in Him, this is His promise for you:

Even the youths shall faint and be weary,
And the young men shall utterly fall,
But those who wait on the LORD
Shall renew their *strength;*
They shall mount up with wings like eagles,
They shall run and not be weary,
They shall walk and not faint.

—Isaiah 40:30–31

Don't feel like you have to be strong right away. The Lord is so gentle and so patient, and He is more than prepared to take this journey with you. He fed Elijah and let him rest before feeding him once more. See the Lord feeding you so gently and so tenderly. And as you meditate on His love and promises for you, I pray that your strength will be renewed like never before.

When You Have No Prayer

Maybe you are at a point where you are so worn down by discouragement you have no strength left to even pray. Maybe like Elijah, you find yourself having no energy to live, and you just want to sleep. Maybe you just feel numb, empty, void of any capacity to feel or do anything. My friend, the Lord doesn't need you to *do* anything. He loves you so much, He has done it all for you. He doesn't need you to compose pretty prayers or to turn up in your "Sunday best" before He helps you. Let me show you something about God:

> *Now it happened in the process of time that the king of Egypt died. Then **the children of Israel groaned because of the bondage,** and they*

*cried out; and their cry came up to God because of the bondage. So **God heard their groaning,** and God remembered His covenant with Abraham, with Isaac, and with Jacob. And God looked upon the children of Israel, and God acknowledged them.*

—Exodus 2:23–25 (boldface mine)

Do you know what God heard? He heard the *groaning* of the Israelites. Even if all you can muster up is a groan, God hears you. Just a groan will reach the throne. Your groan is a prayer that is so powerful because it makes nothing of man's eloquence and religious phraseology, and everything of your need for God's goodness and love. When the bondages in your life and burdens you bear are so heavy that all you can do is groan, your weakness attracts His grace. If you're conscious that you're tired, worn out, and feel helpless, He says to you, "My strength is made perfect in weakness" (2 Cor. 12:9).

Even if all you can muster up is *a groan,* God hears you.

But God didn't just hear the Israelites when they groaned. He also responded with seven "I will's":

"And I have also heard the groaning of the children of Israel whom the Egyptians keep in bondage, and I have remembered My covenant. Therefore say to the children of Israel: 'I am the Lord; **I will** *bring you out from under the burdens of the Egyptians,* **I will** *rescue you from their bondage, and* **I will** *redeem you with an outstretched arm and with great judgments.* **I will** *take you as My people, and* **I will** *be your God. Then you shall know that I am the* Lord *your God who brings you out from under the burdens of the Egyptians. And* **I will** *bring you into the land which I swore to give to Abraham, Isaac, and Jacob; and* **I will** *give it to you as a heritage: I am the* Lord.'"*

—*Exodus 6:5–8 (boldface mine)*

Today, as you simply groan to God, hear Him declaring this to you in whatever situation you are facing:

I will *bring you out from under the burdens you are carrying. Whatever your burdens might be, whether it is the burden of guilt and shame, or the burden of debt, I will bring you out.* **I will** *rescue you from your bondages. Whether the bondages you are facing*

*are due to your own mistakes or pressed upon you
by others, I will rescue you. **I will** redeem you and
ransom you. **I will** take you as My people, and **I
will** be your God. Then you shall know that I am the
Lord your God, who frees you from your oppression.
And **I will** bring you into the land I swore to give to
Abraham, Isaac, and Jacob, and **I will** give it to you
as a heritage. You can boldly receive ALL My promises to you because of what My Son has done [see 2
Cor. 1:20]. I give them all to you as your inheritance
and possession!*

Beloved, these are not just words on a page. The same
Jesus who drew close to Elijah in the day of his depression,
who traversed the Sea of Galilee for the demon-possessed
man, and who walked with the two disciples in their
sadness, is right now drawing close to you. Close your eyes
and see Him coming toward you to wipe away your tears
and bring you out from the burdens you are carrying.
He wants you to cast all your cares, all your anxieties, all
your worries, and all your concerns on Him. Give Him all
your fears, your hurts, your pains, your loneliness, your
depression. And in return, receive His peace that surpasses

human understanding and guards your heart and mind (see Phil. 4:7). That's all God wants you to do. Why? Because He cares about you with deepest affection (see 1 Pet. 5:7 AMP). Because He loves you.

CHAPTER 2

God Is Working Behind the Scenes for You

2

GOD IS *Working* *Behind The Scenes* FOR YOU

I know what it feels like to be under a cloud of oppression. Something happened to my mind when I was a young adult. I read a book that claimed you could lose your salvation if you did not walk in complete obedience to God. Somehow, I believed that and it put me under a terrible bondage that lasted more than a year.

Back then, I did not know about the grace of God and the truth that I was justified by faith alone and not by works. I thought I needed to obey God's laws perfectly. But the more I tried to fully obey all the commandments, the more I fell short and constantly believed I had unforgiven sins. Even if I could control my actions, I could not control my thoughts. It was as though the wrong belief that not all my sins were forgiven had opened the flood-gates in my mind, and my mind became filled with filth and blasphemous thoughts against God. The more I tried to stop them, the more they took control of my mind, and I was convinced I was condemned to hell. I struggled to sleep because I heard voices talking to me and telling me to kill myself.

During that period, I tried everything. Every opportunity I had, I went up to my leaders for prayer. I went for "deliverance sessions" to cast out the "demons" that I wrongly believed were in me. I prayed, I fasted, and I confessed my sins endlessly. I was so sincere about wanting to be right with God that in the midst of conversations with people, I would stop to confess my sin to God if I felt like I had exaggerated a point, or if I thought I had looked at a lady longer than I should have. I took to street evangelism, hoping that if I got more people saved, maybe God would remember me when I was languishing in hell. But no matter what I did, it felt like God had rejected me because I had committed a sin that could never be pardoned. I felt like there was no light, no salvation, and no hope for me.

I am sharing all this with you because I want you to

know that even when you cannot see a way out of your discouragement and depression, there IS hope for you. What you are going through right now might feel like it is going to crush you, but it won't. The enemy is always playing mind games with you, and he wants you to think you are alone in your struggle and that you will never overcome the challenges in your life.

Even when you cannot see a way out of your discouragement and depression, *there is hope* for you.

But the Bible tells us, "No temptation has overtaken you except such as is common to man; but God *is* faithful, who will not allow you to be tempted beyond what you are able, but with the temptation will also make the way of escape, that you may be able to bear *it*" (1 Cor. 10:13). God is faithful, and I believe He has sent me to encourage you. Hold on, my friend, your breakthrough is coming. Hold on, the Lord is your refuge (see Ps. 28:7–8). He will never leave you nor forsake you (see Heb. 13:5). Your story isn't over yet. Keep trusting Him!

Not a Failure Even When You Fail

Coming back to my story, my mind was so riddled with uncontrollable thoughts that it felt like it would snap at any moment, but it didn't. I survived. And not only did I survive, I am now living a life in Christ that is truly exceedingly, abundantly, above all that I could imagine (see Eph. 3:20). The enemy tried to bring me down, but the Lord saved me. I do not deserve any of the blessings I am enjoying, nor can I ever earn the unimaginable goodness of His grace toward me. But today, He is using me—this formerly oppressed man who was a stammerer and stutterer when He picked me up—to preach around the world the good news about the finished work of Jesus Christ. And I will keep preaching until there is no breath left in me because this life that I am living is not mine but His.

I will keep proclaiming that *of Him we are in Christ Jesus*, who became for us wisdom, righteousness, sanctification, and redemption, because this was the verse that God used to break me free from my mental oppression (see 1 Cor. 1:30). I pray that this verse will minister to you too as you see yourself IN Christ. Those who are in Christ are new creations (see 2 Cor. 5:17). Those who are in

Christ are blessed with every blessing (see Eph. 1:3). Those who are in Christ are safe and protected in the secret place of the Most High (see Ps. 91:1). Christ Himself is our wisdom, our righteousness, our sanctification, and our redemption!

It was God who placed you and me *in Christ*. No one can take us out—not even ourselves. Once we have invited Jesus into our lives, we can never lose our salvation (see John 10:28). "Neither death nor life, nor angels nor principalities nor powers, nor things present nor things to come, nor height nor depth, nor any other created thing, shall be able to separate us from the love of God which is in Christ Jesus our Lord" (Rom. 8:38–39). The moment we accepted Christ as our Lord and Savior, all ours sins—past, present, and future—were completely forgiven (see Eph. 1:7, Col. 2:13). Though our sins were as scarlet, the blood of Jesus has washed us whiter than snow (see Isa. 1:18).

I will keep preaching the good news that we are saved by grace through faith, and there is nothing we can do to earn His blessings, because it has nothing to do with us and everything to do with His undeserved, unmerited favor (see Eph. 2:8). I will keep announcing that even when we fail, God does not see us in our failures, He sees us *in Christ*. We can come boldly to God because as Christ is, so are we in this world (see 1 John 4:17). As Christ is completely holy and blameless, so are we! Why? Because He who knew no sin became sin for us, that we might become the righteousness of God in Him (see 2 Cor. 5:21)!

Knowing that we are completely forgiven and irrevocably saved is so important to our mental well-being and putting a stop to the enemy's mind games. I've shared with you how having a wrong belief in this area brought me into depression. Some years ago, I met a renowned psychiatrist when I was preaching in Palermo, Italy. He told me he had countless patients who had been committed to mental care institutions because they did not believe their sins were forgiven and struggled with guilt and condemnation. He told me that many in his profession would be out of a job if people truly believed their sins were forgiven and their salvation was secure. That made me want to preach even more strongly on the grace of our Lord Jesus Christ so that more will come to know Him and understand the perfection of His work on the cross!

God Is Working Behind the Scenes

I want to show you something from the life of Jacob that I pray will help you catch a glimpse of just how good God is, and why you can trust Him even when your situation appears bleak. Genesis 37 records how Jacob had mourned for many days because he believed his son, Joseph, whom he loved "more than all his children" (Gen. 37:3), had been devoured by wild beasts. He refused to be comforted and said, "For I shall go down into the grave to my son in mourning" (Gen. 37:35).

Maybe you are mourning a loss in your life right now, and it feels like the pain will never stop till you die. It could be the death of a loved one, or perhaps the death of a dream you had worked many years for. I know the pain can feel like it is too much to bear, but keep trusting the Lord, my friend.

Well, years passed and Genesis 42 records how Jacob sent ten of his sons to Egypt to buy grain because a severe famine had stripped the land of food. When they were there, the governor of Egypt accused them of being spies and detained one of the brothers, Simeon, and demanded that the rest go back and bring their youngest brother, Benjamin, to prove that they were telling the truth. When they got back to their father and told him what had happened and how the governor wanted Benjamin, Jacob cried out, "You have bereaved me: Joseph is no *more*, Simeon is no *more*, and you want to take Benjamin. **All these things are against me**" (Gen. 42:36, boldface mine).

Perhaps that is the cry in your heart right now. Maybe you are looking at the challenges in your life, and you are asking, "Lord, what happened to Your promises?" Maybe it feels like everything in your life is against you. But I want to announce to you that whatever may be happening in your life, these things are *not* against you. Your God has gone ahead of you to prepare a place for you that is greater than where you are right now. Jacob despaired because he looked at the lack of food and loss of his son. If only he had known that God was working behind the scenes for him. If only he had known that the governor of Egypt was actually his beloved Joseph, who was alive, and that because of Joseph, his whole family would be well provided for even in the midst of famine (see Gen. 45).

All Things Will Work Together for Your Good

My friend, open your eyes. The Lord Jesus—your heavenly Joseph—is working out everything for you. Soon, you will be rejoicing. Soon, you will see that all the things that look like they are against you are actually *for* you. He is causing ALL things to work together for your good (see Rom. 8:28). That means even when negative things happen to you—things that are painful and that cause you to cry till you have no tears left—God can cause them to work together for your good!

He is causing *all things* to work together for your good!

I want to show you what Joseph said to his brothers, who had thrown him into a pit, sold him as a slave, and lied to their father to make him think he was dead:

"But now, do not therefore be grieved or angry with yourselves because you sold me here; for God sent me before you to preserve life. . . .God sent me before you to preserve a posterity for you in the earth, and to save your lives by a great deliverance. So now it

was *not you* who *sent me here, but God; and He has made me a father to Pharaoh, and lord of all his house, and a ruler throughout all the land of Egypt."*

—*Genesis 45:5–8*

Who would have known that God was orchestrating things behind the scenes? It certainly would not have looked that way to Joseph when he found himself, years before, stripped bare and paraded in a slave market, or when he was thrown into prison because of a false accusation against him (see Gen. 39:1, 19–20). It certainly did not look that way to Jacob when he held Joseph's blood-soaked tunic in his hands (see Gen. 37:33).

But through it all, God was in control and causing all things to work together for Joseph's good. Every trouble that Joseph encountered, from the pit to the prison, was actually a stepping-stone to bring him closer to where God wanted him to be. Joseph's brothers meant evil against him, but God used all that happened to position Joseph, and to save not just Joseph—but also his whole family—by a great deliverance.

No matter how dire your circumstances appear, the battle is _not over_ until you see your victory in Christ!

My friend, whatever you might be going through today, know that God is with you, and He is working things out for your good. No matter how dire your circumstances appear, the battle is not over until you see your victory in Christ!

Shouldn't Believers Have Trial-Free Lives?

Some people erroneously think that if you are a believer you should not have to go through any trials, so they get disappointed with God when they face challenges in their lives. The truth is, Jesus tells us in John 16:33 that in this life "you will have tribulation." But the verse does not stop there. It goes on to say that even in the midst of the trials, we can be of good cheer, because our Lord Jesus has overcome the world!

Deuteronomy 28:1–13 is all about His blessings, and yet verse 7 says, "The LORD will cause your enemies who rise against you to be defeated before your face; they shall come out against you one way and flee before you seven ways." What does this tell you? Even when His blessings are upon you, there will still be enemies who will rise against you. But when they do, guess what? You don't have to fear your enemies or run away from the challenges that confront you. As a child of God, you can face your enemies boldly because God will defeat them before your face. Right there, in the presence (not absence) of your enemies, God will prepare a table before you (see Ps. 23:5).

No matter how big your challenges may be, your God is *even bigger*. And if God is for you, who or what can be against you (see Rom. 8:31)? Whatever or whomever the enemy might be, it might come against you one way, but God will cause all your enemies to be scattered before you seven ways!

Out of Your Battles Will Come Spoils for You

And that's not all. Because you are a child of God, the Bible promises that when you go through a battle, God will bring you out greater, stronger, and healthier than before you went through the trial. If you know your rights and inheritance as a child of God, you don't have to fear any battle. David and his men went through many battles, but the Bible tells us, "Out of the spoils won in battles did they dedicate to maintain the house of the LORD" (1 Chron. 26:27 KJV).

When you keep your eyes *on the Lord,* you will come out from your battle with greater blessings than before!

What battle are you in today? Are you struggling with anxious, fearful, or suicidal thoughts? Are you addicted to medication or drugs? Is your marriage facing a crisis? Take heart and know this: Out of your battles will come spoils for you. When you keep your eyes on the Lord, you will come out from your battle with greater blessings than before!

Much More Will Be Restored to You

In the Scriptures, there is a law of restoration that says:

"If a man steals an ox or a sheep, and slaughters it or

sells it, he shall restore five oxen for an ox and four
sheep for a sheep."

—Exodus 22:1

You have an enemy—a thief who comes to steal, and to kill, and to destroy (see John 10:10). But for everything he steals or takes from you, God restores many times more what the enemy has stolen.

Perhaps the enemy has stolen your health, and you have been plagued with a long-term condition. Perhaps your self-esteem and confidence have been robbed by things that have happened to you. My friend, do not be discouraged. You have a God who made this promise to you: "I will repay two blessings for each of your troubles" (Zech. 9:12 NLT). Whatever has been stolen from you, whatever troubles you might be going through, God doesn't just give you what was taken from you—He will restore much more to you.

God Can Turn Your Evil Day into Good Days

Maybe it feels like the enemy is determined to destroy you and all that is dear to you. You might be on the brink of bankruptcy, or your home may have been destroyed by a natural disaster. Whatever your situation, God can turn things around for you.

During the reign of King Ahasuerus, a powerful official named Haman plotted to kill a Jew named Mordecai who had offended him, as well as all the Jews in the empire. But on the day that the enemies of the Jews had hoped to eradicate them, the opposite occurred (see Esther 9:1). The Jews defeated all their enemies. In fact, even before that, Haman was hanged on the very gallows he had prepared for Mordecai (see Esther 7:10). It was better for Haman not to have come against Mordecai. Likewise, it is better for the enemy not to have come against you.

Our God is the God of the turnaround, and He will turn your situation around. He's the God of Esther, He's the God of Mordecai, and He is your God. Right now, He is preparing to turn your day of mourning into a day of joy, your evil day into a day of gladness. If the enemy has told you there is no way out of your misery, he's lying. Your evil day is coming to an end, and your day of gladness, dawning!

You Can Come Out of Your Trial Stronger

In my own life, I saw how the Lord turned things completely around for me, and I will forever be grateful that He did. But as much as I never want to go through that darkness and depression again, I also believe that if the enemy had not attacked my mind the way he did, I would not have learned all about the Lord's goodness and be preaching so unapologetically about His life-transforming, bondage-breaking grace all around the world. The enemy tried to destroy me, but the Lord saved me, and I came out so much stronger than before. And I am humbled that He didn't just save me—He has used my ministry to help so many others, and I give Him all the glory!

Healed of Severe Depression, Anxiety, and Insomnia

My team and I have received many testimonies over the years from people who have received breakthroughs as they listened to my preaching and read my books. I'll just share one here. If you are suffering from depression, I would like you to read Mike's testimony in his own words, and I pray you will be encouraged:

For two years, I suffered severe depression, anxiety, and insomnia. Going to general practitioners, psychologists, and psychiatrists didn't help and I had to rely on sleeping pills, antidepressants, and anti-anxiety tablets.

While walking past a bookstore one day, Pastor Prince's book The Power of Right Believing *caught my attention. When I read the words "chronic depression" on its back cover, I knew the book dealt with one of the problems I had, and I decided to get it.*

I started on the book immediately when I got home. To my astonishment, it was completely different from all the faith-based books I'd read before. Pastor Prince addressed my depression, anxiety, and sleeplessness as though he knew me personally. Each and every page also said something profound about my struggles.

I kept on reading and have never looked back since. It has opened my eyes to the love of our Lord and Savior, Jesus Christ. I also prayed the prayer on page 146 that says:

> *"Thank You, Jesus, for loving me. Today I receive Your complete forgiveness in my life, and I forgive myself for all my sins, mistakes, and failings. I release them all into Your loving hands. I declare that in You, I am completely forgiven, free, accepted, favored, righteous, blessed, and healed from every sickness and disease. Amen!"*

> *Today, I am completely healed. I can even fall asleep without sleeping pills. Praise the name of Jesus!*

Hallelujah! I rejoice with Mike over the freedom and joy he is walking in today. The Lord set him free from his depression, anxiety, and sleeplessness, and He can also set you free from the bondages you are under.

If you are going through a difficult season right now, and the enemy has been stealing from you, whether it's your joy, your finances, your health, or your relationships, get ready. God is with you, and He is working things out for you. Everything that has been taken from you—whatever you have been robbed, defrauded, cheated of, be it by man or the devil—God will restore. Your restoration is on the way and the Lord will restore to you so much more than what the enemy has stolen from you! The challenges and attacks in your life may be painful, but do not let them bring you down. Don't let the enemy deceive you anymore. I am praying for you and believing with you that God will cause your situation to turn around, and that out of your battles will come spoils for you!

CHAPTER 3

Don't Let the Enemy Mess with You

3

DON'T LET THE ENEMY MESS WITH YOU

Are you struggling with negative thoughts that cripple you and maybe even cause you to feel suicidal? Thoughts like, *I should give up and stop being a burden to others,* or *I'm all alone and nobody cares if I'm even alive.* Thoughts like, *There is no hope for me—things will never get better.* Or, *I am worthless and it's better for everyone if I just disappeared.* If you have been having such thoughts that cause you to spiral downwards, I pray you will see that those are not thoughts from God—they are lies from the pit of hell.

The enemy is a master of mind games. His modus operandi is to plant lies in your head because he knows that if he can control your thoughts, he can manipulate your emotions. It is what he did in the Garden of Eden when he lied to Adam and Eve to cause them to harbor wrong beliefs about God, and it is what he continues to do today. The enemy is known as the accuser (see Rev. 12:10), and he is constantly accusing you to make you feel like you have not done enough and are not good enough—not good enough as a minister, a parent, or even as a Christian. He puts thoughts in your mind that cause you to focus only on negative things about yourself—your past, your failures, the seemingly endless demands put on you, the job you lost, how rejected you feel.

Stop listening to his lies. I may not know what you have gone through or the areas where you have failed, but I do know you have a God who loves you, and He has good plans for you, plans to give you a future and a hope (see Jer. 29:11). I do know the Lord calls you the apple of His eye (see Zech. 2:8), and He delights in you (see Zeph. 3:17 NLT). I do know our Lord Jesus has paid the price for you to be freed from the oppressive thoughts that bind you. In fact, I believe the first area He redeemed us from is the area of our thoughts.

Before Jesus was scourged for our diseases and crucified for our sins, He first shed His blood for us—from the brow of His head—in the Garden of Gethsemane. When Adam sinned, God said to him, "By the sweat of your brow you will eat your food" (Gen. 3:19 NIV). What happened in the Garden of Eden was ended in another garden by our Lord Jesus, the second Adam, when He was under such duress that He sweat blood. The Gospel of Luke records what happened: "And being in agony he prayed more earnestly: and his sweat was as it were great drops of blood falling down to the ground" (Luke 22:44 KJV).

Research has shown that the capillary blood vessels that feed the sweat glands can rupture when one is under conditions of extreme physical or emotional stress, causing blood to be secreted.[1] As Jesus shed blood from His brow, His blood redeemed you from every thought that robs you of joy and victory. It redeemed you from your stress, worries, fears, and anxieties!

Why You Can Be Free of Dark and Deadly Thoughts

But Jesus did not stop there. He allowed Himself to be arrested, beaten, and scourged. After He had been savagely scourged, the Roman soldiers put a scarlet robe on Him.

They twisted a crown of thorns and forced it on His head. They ridiculed Him, mocked Him, and spat on Him. They struck His head again and again with a reed, ramming the thorns into His head (see Matt. 27:27–30). And He allowed those thorns, which represent the curse (see Gen. 3:17–18), to sink into His brow, so that He could bear your curse of depression, despair, pessimism, and anxiety.

Jesus endured the shame and pain, so that you can be filled with His joy. And after all that, He allowed Himself to be crucified. Do you know where Jesus was crucified? It was at Golgotha, which means "Place of a Skull" (Matt. 27:33). The skull represents your thinking, and it also represents death. I believe one of the reasons He was crucified at Golgotha is that the place represents our dark and deadly thinking, and His sacrifice there allows us to be free from negative, destructive thoughts.

Stop believing the lies the enemy wants you to believe about yourself.

You are *so* loved by Jesus. Stop despising and hurting yourself. Stop believing the lies the enemy wants you to believe about yourself. Stop allowing him to play games with your mind. Stop allowing depression and despair to cloud your thoughts. Choose to fix your thoughts on Jesus and allow Him to keep you in His perfect peace (see Isa. 26:3 NLT). Whatever you might be going through, whatever areas you have failed in, you can wake up each morning with hope, thinking, *Give thanks to the LORD, for* He is *good!* (Ps. 118:29). Because of the blood of Jesus, you can receive the peace of God that surpasses all understanding, the peace of God that guards your heart and mind through Christ Jesus (see Phil. 4:7)!

Jesus Heals Your Broken Heart

The Lord loves you so much. A divine exchange took place when He went to the cross. He who knew no sin became sin so that you might become the righteousness of God in Him (see 2 Cor. 5:21). He became a curse so that you might receive His blessings (see Gal. 3:13–14). Whatever Jesus bore on the cross, you do not have to bear today. In Christ, you are redeemed from every curse of the law, from every penalty for your sins. He bore your pains and sicknesses and carried your sorrows so that you might be filled with His divine health (see Isa. 53:4). He became poor so that through His poverty you can always have more than enough (see 2 Cor. 8:9). He became "a man of sorrows, acquainted with deepest grief" (Isa. 53:3 NLT), so that you might receive His joy. And you might not know this, but His heart was broken, so that yours might be whole.

Maybe you have suffered a miscarriage, or a loved one has passed away, and you cannot stop crying. Maybe your husband left you, and you feel utterly shattered and betrayed. Maybe you've given so much to your family or to your job, only to find yourself uncared for and discarded as you've gotten older. Whatever has broken your heart and caused the deep, unyielding sadness that is overwhelming you, the Lord wants you to know you are not alone in your pain.

The Bible tells us, "The LORD is close to the brokenhearted and saves those who are crushed in spirit" (Ps. 34:18 NIV). He is so close to you right now, and He wants to take away the grief, hurt, and disappointment that have devastated you. The same God who calls each star by name knows you by name and wants to heal your broken heart and bind up your wounds (see Ps. 147:3–4). I know it feels like your heart will never be whole again, but I pray that as you look away from your pain, and behold instead His wonderful love for you, strength will flow through you, and the oil of His joy will be a healing balm for your wounds.

I want to show you a passage of Scripture that captures God's heart for you so beautifully. May it allow you to catch a glimpse of why God sent our Lord Jesus:

"The Spirit of the Lord GOD is upon Me,
Because the LORD has anointed Me
To preach good tidings to the poor;
He has sent Me to heal the brokenhearted,
To proclaim liberty to the captives,
And the opening of the prison to those who
  are bound;
To proclaim the acceptable year of the LORD,
And the day of vengeance of our God;
To comfort all who mourn,
To console those who mourn in Zion,
To give them beauty for ashes,
The oil of joy for mourning,
The garment of praise for the spirit of heaviness;

That they may be called trees of righteousness,

*The planting of the L*ORD*, that He may be glorified."*

And they shall rebuild the old ruins,

They shall raise up the former desolations,

And they shall repair the ruined cities,

The desolations of many generations.

—Isaiah 61:1–4

Our Lord Jesus was sent to heal your broken heart. The people around you may not even know you are hurting. All they see are your smiles and the outward success you seem to have. But even when you try to hide your pain from those around you, He sees it. He knows that "laughter can conceal a heavy heart, but when the laughter ends, the grief remains" (Prov. 14:13 NLT). He sees you as you are, and He sees you as you struggle against the loneliness, hurt, and pain in your life. He knows what you are going through, and He knows the things that bring depression in your secret moments, the things that nobody else knows.

He Sees Your Struggle and Comes to You

The Gospel of Mark records what happened when Jesus

was alone on a mountain one evening to pray. His disciples were in a boat in the middle of the sea, but "**He saw them** straining at rowing, for the wind was against them" (Mark 6:48, boldface mine). And do you know what He did? He *came to them*, walking on the water.

Right now, I pray that the Lord will cause your spiritual eyes to open so that you can see Him coming to you in the midst of your storm. The enemy wants you to keep looking at yourself—your pain, your failures, the things that have happened to you. Look away. The more you focus on them, the more you will sink deeper and deeper into despair. But as you behold Him who is Master over the wind and waves, you become like Him (see 2 Cor. 3:18). As long as Peter kept his eyes on Jesus and not the storm, he walked on water (see Matt. 14:22–33).

Beloved, keep your eyes on the Lord even when your heart is hurting, even when you have questions that cannot be answered. Choose to lean on His love for you. You might think you are facing the storm alone, but just as He saw His disciples straining against the storm, He sees you struggling. If somewhere in your heart you have believed that God has abandoned you because you are discouraged, that is a lie from the enemy. Nothing could be further from the truth. He loves you, sees your struggle, and is coming to you even now.

Why You Don't Have to Endure Bullying and Shame

Do you know what our Lord Jesus did to heal your broken heart? He allowed His own heart to be broken. Psalm 69 is a Messianic psalm that depicts our Lord Jesus on the cross. In verse 20, it says this:

> *Reproach has broken my heart, and I am full of heaviness; I looked for someone to take pity, but there was none; and for comforters, but I found none.*
>
> —*Psalm 69:20*

This verse tells us that "reproach" broke Jesus' heart. The Hebrew word for "reproach" is *cherpah*, meaning scorn, taunting, disgrace, rebuke, and shame.[2] Perhaps there are people in your life who have been taunting and shaming you. It could be your parents, your spouse, the people in your school or at your workplace, or even your adult children saying things about you that cause you to feel ashamed, worthless, or dirty. Maybe it seems like everyone around you is picking on you and despising you. Today, we call it bullying, and we know that being a victim of bullying can cause you to fall into depression.[3] If you are being bullied, don't stay silent. Please talk to someone you trust. I'm praying that the Lord will help you to find the help and support you need.

At the same time, I want you to know that on the cross, our Lord Jesus bore the hurtful words people have spoken toward you. He bore every insult, every ridicule, and every scorn. The reproach that broke His heart was your reproach. The rejection that broke His heart at the cross was your rejection. From now on, guard your heart—whenever someone scorns or ridicules you, imagine Jesus absorbing it for you, bearing all your hurt and shame on the cross. See Him allowing His heart to be broken in place of yours. I also want you to see that Isaiah 61:7 declares, "Instead of your shame *you shall have* double *honor.*" That's His promise to you. He took your shame so that you can receive double honor.

His Heart Was Broken so Yours Can Be Whole

After Jesus had died on the cross, a soldier thrust a spear into His side to confirm His death, and the Bible records that "blood and water came out" (John 19:34). According to some Bible scholars and medical researchers, Jesus likely developed pulmonary edema and pericardial effusion (the build-up of fluid around the lungs and heart) as He struggled to breathe on the cross.[4] In severe cases of cardiac stress, cardiac rupture can happen and the heart bursts. I believe that is what happened to our Lord Jesus— He literally died of a broken heart. He has paid the price.

Beloved, lift up your head. Step out of your ashes and receive His beauty. Give Him your mourning and take His oil of joy. Give Him your spirit of heaviness and put on His garment of praise. See Him coming to you and comforting you in the midst of your mourning. If you have been bound by oppressive thoughts and imprisoned by discouragement and despair, the Lord declares liberty to you today. Maybe you have been bound by drugs, pornography, unclean habits, or depression. Whatever you are bound by, He has come to proclaim freedom to you. Whatever areas of brokenness there might be in your life, the Lord declares that the old ruins shall be rebuilt and former desolations shall be raised up (see Isa. 61:4).

Because you are in Christ, there is hope. You are loved. You are loved. You are loved!

A Prayer for the Hurting

If you know depressive thoughts have bound you or your heart has been broken, I want to invite you to pray the prayer below. As you pray, may the God of peace crush Satan under your feet and cause you to walk in a whole new level of hope and freedom, in Jesus' mighty name.

Lord Jesus, thank You for loving me. Thank You for bearing my reproaches, my pain, my shame, and my rejections. I give You all the bitterness, anger, and resentment that have imprisoned me for so long. I give You the pain that has broken my heart and caused me to feel hopeless. I open my heart to You, and I receive Your love for me that was demonstrated at the cross. In all the areas I feel unworthy, in all the areas I have believed the lies of the enemy and allowed him to poison my mind, I thank You that right now, You are uprooting those lies. Help me to receive Your love and to walk in the liberty that You purchased for me to enjoy. In Your name I pray, Amen.

CHAPTER 4

Practical Keys to Break Free

4

PRACTICAL KEYS TO
Break Free

The enemy wants you shrouded in depression and trapped in a stronghold of hopelessness and pessimism. He wants to blind you with his lies so that even when there is good in your life, you cannot see it (see Jer. 17:6). He wants to rob you of the ability to hope so that you believe things will only get worse. Maybe he has succeeded in making you feel worthless and inadequate. Maybe he has planted the lie that the people around you would be happier when you are gone. Maybe you are entertaining thoughts of suicide because you are so tired and discouraged you have no strength to carry on. But don't allow him to play mind games with you anymore. God wants to take you out of the darkness and put you into His wonderful light (see

1 Pet. 2:9). You have so much to live for because God has a glorious future for you.

Reach Out to Godly People

If depression and anxiety have immobilized you, and you find yourself entertaining thoughts of suicide, please reach out to someone you trust. Reach out to friends who are believers, a Christian counselor, or leaders in your church. Talk to them about what you are going through, and get them to pray with you. Maybe you do not want to talk to anyone because you think, *Nobody understands me*, or, *If I tell others what I am going through, they will despise me.*

Beloved, those are lies the devil uses to cut you off from others. Don't allow the enemy to separate you from the people around you because that's when he will begin to take you into a dark, downward spiral. He wants you to cut yourself off from human contact because he knows that when all you have is your own perceived inadequacies and challenges, you will sink deeper and deeper into despair.

God can use people to bring His Word to you. That is why the enemy is so bent on isolating you. Over and over again, the Bible records how God puts His words into the mouths of people (see Deut. 18:18, Isa. 51:16, Jer. 1:9, Luke 12:12). Please allow godly people into your life and give them the opportunity to minister words of life to you. Let the Lord use them to expose the enemy's lies. Let the Lord use them to impart strength to you. Let the Lord use them to love you. You are so precious to Him, and He loves you so much.

Allow godly people into your life and give them the opportunity to minister *words of life* to you.

When your faith runs low, let someone else help you and carry you to Jesus. The Gospel of Mark tells the story of four men who broke through the roof to bring a paralytic to Jesus (see Mark 2:1–12). It records that "Jesus saw their faith" and healed the paralyzed man. You were not meant to be alone. Solomon, the wisest man who ever lived, wrote, "Two people are better off than one. . . .If one person falls, the other can reach out and help" (Eccl. 4:9–10 NLT).

So don't allow the enemy to keep you away from

people. Go to a care group or invite the most encouraging friends you know to have coffee with you. Sometimes the problems in your life can cause you to despair because you see no way out. Talking to godly people can give you different perspectives and help you to see God in your situation. The enemy wants you to feel ashamed for asking for help, but the Bible tells us that "in the multitude of counselors *there is* safety" (Prov. 11:14). There is wisdom in asking for help.

Be Planted in the House

If you don't already belong to a church, can I encourage you to join a church that points you to the goodness and faithfulness of our God, and to immerse yourself in a community of faith? The Bible tells us, "Those who are planted in the house of the LORD shall flourish in the courts of our God" (Ps. 92:13). My friend, I want to see you flourishing, not wasting away under the weight of discouragement. Don't drift from one church to another, or simply turn up in church without making connections with anyone else— be planted and rooted.

Plant yourself in a church by joining a ministry or

small group where you can get to know other believers and allow your pastors and leaders to water you constantly with the Word. When you allow your spiritual shepherds to speak anointed words over you that can destroy the yoke of despair and discouragement over your life (see Isa. 10:27 KJV), the Lord promises that you shall fear no more, nor be dismayed, nor lack in any area (see Jer. 23:4).

Start Doing Things

Maybe depression has paralyzed you so that every day, you just want to shut yourself up in your room and stay in bed all day with your curtains drawn. When you are suffering from depression, you may feel constantly fatigued and lose interest in doing things you once enjoyed. Your sleep may be affected, and you may find yourself eating too much or not having any appetite at all. Regardless of how you feel, can I encourage you not to allow the enemy to immobilize you any longer? Start taking small steps by faith, even if your flesh does not feel like doing it. And don't worry if you don't see a transformation in yourself immediately.

When Jesus explained the parable of the farmer scattering seed, He said, "The seed that fell on good soil represents those who hear and accept God's word and produce a harvest of thirty, sixty, or even a hundred times as much as had been planted!" (Mark 4:20 NLT). As you keep receiving God's Word or seed into your heart, you will see change. You may not see an overnight transformation, but keep moving forward. Keep going by faith and not by sight, and you will start to see some results—first the thirtyfold, then the sixtyfold, and eventually the hundredfold!

You can start breaking the stronghold of depression by getting yourself up from your bed and going outdoors for a walk. Researchers have found that there is a link between depression and the lack of exposure to sunlight.[1] Our Lord Jesus walked a lot and often went into the wilderness or up into the mountains to pray. I think there's just something about being outdoors—surrounded by the majesty and beauty of His creation—that can help us to look beyond our problems and ourselves.

If you're living in the city, just take a walk down the blocks and as you do, talk to your heavenly Father. You don't need to craft eloquent prayers, just tell Him all that's on your heart. You can also pour out your heart to Him on a park bench. If you have no words, just cry in His presence. Your weeping is not in vain (see Ps. 126:5–6 NIV). Whatever you might be going through, know that He will carry you through it all and bring you to a place of abundance and strength (see Ps. 66:12 AMP).

Start doing things that you know the enemy wants to stop you from doing. He might have formed the weapon of depression against you, but it shall not prosper (see Isa. 54:17)! Do something that makes you laugh, because "a merry heart does good, *like* medicine" (Prov. 17:22). If you can, start exercising or take up a sport even if you don't feel like doing so, as the Bible tells us that "physical training is good" (1 Tim. 4:8 NLT). And even as you are still waiting for your breakthrough, start praising Him. Our Lord Jesus came to give you "the garment of praise for the spirit of heaviness" (Isa. 61:3). As you sing praises to Him and worship Him, I pray that His Spirit will liberate you and drive away every worry and concern that is weighing you down (see 2 Cor. 3:17).

Stop Comparing Yourself with Others

We live in an age when people are comparing themselves

against others like never before. When you go on social media, you are bombarded by pictures of the seemingly perfect lives that everybody else lives, and there is even a counter to measure how many people "like" you. The enemy uses comparison to plant lies in your head, lies that your life is pathetic compared to others, that you are a lousy parent, and that everyone else is better than you.

Constant comparison breeds discouragement because the enemy will always point out how you pale in comparison. Stop comparing yourself against others. Stop going on social media if it affects you. If you want to know how much you are worth, just look at the price God paid to redeem you. He gave up heaven's best—Jesus—for you. You are made in the image of God Himself, and He calls you the apple of His eye!

Hear Right and Be Healed

Maybe you are in need of healing from a physical condition, or you have been struggling with a mental condition for years. Or maybe your condition cannot be diagnosed and treated by doctors because it is a pain that comes from having a broken heart. Whatever healing you need, I want to show you a divine order that is captured in the Bible:

> However, the report went around concerning Him
> all the more; and great multitudes came together **to
> hear, and to be healed** by Him of their infirmities.
> —*Luke 5:15 (boldface mine)*

Notice that the people didn't just come to Jesus to be healed. They came to *hear* Him, and then they were healed. Hear and be healed. Keep hearing the preaching of His Word. Even if you don't see your healing taking place immediately, keep hearing. We have received so many testimonies from precious people around the world who received healing for various conditions just by listening to the preached Word. Hearing is so important because "faith *comes* by hearing, and hearing by the word of God" (Rom. 10:17).

If you need healing in any area of your life, don't just ask for prayer. Make sure you are hearing all that God has to say about healing. Proverbs 4:22 tells us that God's words are "life to those who find them, and health to all their flesh." Many medications treat one part of your body, only to cause side effects elsewhere. Only the Word of God is health to *all* your flesh. Make sure what you are hearing doesn't just consist of negative reports from your doctor, the news media, or the stock market. Start listening to preaching that tells you all about what Jesus has done on the cross for you!

God's words are life to those who find them, and *health to all their flesh.*

I really believe there's something special about listening to the preached Word, and I want to bless you with a message that will greatly encourage you today if you are struggling with discouragement and depression. To hear it, just log on to JosephPrince.com/winover to download the free audio message *Win over Discouragement, Depression and Burnout*. I know this resource will help you receive a powerful impartation from the Lord that will cause you to win your battle with discouragement.

Look Away from Your Challenges

I pray that you have received a fresh revelation of Jesus that will allow you to *trust* Him, even when you can't *see* your breakthrough yet. Be more conscious of your invisible God than the things that are visible. Being conscious of your challenges will not resolve them in any way. Focusing on your mounting debts will not cause them to disappear, nor will thinking about that fractured relationship or that alcohol dependency improve your situation. The Bible puts it this way: "Which of you by worrying can add one cubit to his stature?" (Matt. 6:27). But something supernatural can happen when you choose to look away from your problems and look to your Solution instead.

The Bible teaches us what to do when overwhelming difficulties surround us. There's a passage in Numbers 21 that tells us what happened after fiery serpents bit the Israelites in the wilderness and many of them died. The account shows you that whether your body is fighting a disease, your mind is oppressed with depression, or your marital life is breaking down, God has provided the answer. Many probably believe that the answer lies in removing the cause of the problem, and that's what the Israelites wanted. They prayed for the serpents to be taken away. Maybe you have prayed the same prayer yourself, and asked God to take away the chronic pain in your body or to remove your financial debt. But look at what God told Moses to do:

> "*Make a fiery* serpent, *and set it on a pole; and it*
> *shall be that everyone who is bitten, when he looks at*
> *it, shall live.*"
>
> *—Numbers 21:8*

So Moses made a bronze serpent and put it on a pole, "and so it was, if a serpent had bitten anyone, when he looked at the bronze serpent, he lived" (Num. 21:9). Do you know what God is talking about? Bronze in the Bible speaks of judgment. In the Old Testament, the altar of burnt offering, where the animal sacrifices were burned to atone for Israel's sins, was overlaid with bronze (see Exod. 27:1–2).

In the Gospel of John, Jesus said, "And as Moses lifted up the serpent in the wilderness, even so must the Son of Man be lifted up" (John 3:14). So the bronze serpent is a picture of our Lord Jesus, judged and punished on the cross with every consequence of our sins. Sickness and death are part of the punishment. Poverty is part of the punishment. But Christ bore them all for us, and that means these things no longer have any right to afflict us!

Focus on His Finished Work on the Cross

Just as God wanted the Israelites to look away from their painful snakebites and to look at the bronze serpent, He wants us to look away from our trials and from ourselves, and to look instead at His provision on the cross. The Hebrew word used for "looked" in Numbers 21:9 is *nabat*, which means to "look intently at."[2] Whether we have been bitten by debt, disease, or discouragement, our answer lies in looking intently and expectantly at Jesus' finished work on the cross.

Even when the "fiery serpents" are still around us, and even when we can feel the pain from the bites we have received, God's answer is to look at the bronze serpent on the pole. To look at the bronze serpent means that we cannot at the same time be looking and focusing on the snakes around us and the wounds that we have suffered. We have to keep our eyes on our Lord Jesus, who was crucified for all our sins. Whatever area you are struggling in, ask God for a fresh revelation of Jesus. As we've read in Numbers 21:8–9, the promise is that "everyone" and "anyone" who looks shall receive a breakthrough!

Sit at Jesus' Feet and Hear His Word

Maybe you find yourself crying out, "God, don't You care what I am going through?" Maybe you're asking Him, "Don't You care that my child is suffering?" or "Don't You care that I'm all alone?" If that is the cry of your heart today, I want you to see our Lord Jesus' response to Martha, who said to Him, "Lord, do You not care that my sister has left me to serve alone?" Jesus lovingly said to her, "Martha, Martha, you are worried and troubled about many things. But **one thing is needed**, and Mary has chosen that good part" (Luke 10:40–42, boldface mine).

Do you know what the "one thing" that Mary did was? She sat at Jesus' feet and heard His Word.

When you are overwhelmed by many things—responsibilities, demands, and challenges—the enemy will often come in to plant the lie that God does not care about you and that you are all alone in managing the issues of your life. That's not the time to cut yourself off from God like the enemy wants you to. The same Jesus who said, "Come to Me, all *you* who labor and are heavy laden" (Matt. 11:28), wants you to come to Him and hear His Word. Even if you do not feel like doing it, do something to get

His Word into you, whether it's listening to sermons or reading the Bible or a daily devotional. I truly believe that when you do this one thing needful, He will lead you to success and stability in all areas of your life, be it your marriage, ministry, career, or physical and mental health.

Arm Yourself with God's Word

Getting a hold of God's Word is so important especially when you are in a war against the enemy. Allow the Lord to build you up and strengthen you with His Word. Gird yourself with truth and learn to counter every lie and attack from the enemy with the sword of the Word of God (see Eph. 6:14–17). The enemy knows how powerful the Word is and that is why Jesus tells us that the enemy comes *immediately* to steal the Word before it can take root in your life (see Mark 4:15).

During the earlier years of our church's growth, I found myself concerned about finding a permanent location for our services. God led me to a verse in the book of Ruth, and with that verse, I fought all the battles of anxieties, worries, and cares I had about securing a venue.

Whatever you are fighting, find verses you can meditate on and declare over your situation. For instance, if the enemy has been attacking your sleep, declare Psalm 127:2—"He gives His beloved sleep." If you are struggling to make ends meet, declare, "And my God shall supply all your need according to His riches in glory by Christ Jesus" (Phil. 4:19). If you do not know where to begin, I have listed down some verses (on pages 81 to 107) that I pray will bless you and help you overcome every lie of the enemy and every challenge you might be facing.

Don't Give Up, There Is Hope!

Beloved, the enemy wants you to think there is no hope for you. He wants you to feel hopeless, helpless, and useless. But I want you to know that the Bible calls God "the God of hope" (Rom. 15:13). This "hope" in the New Testament is *a confident expectation of good*.[3] As long as you have God, you have hope. With the God of hope in your life, you can always expect a bright future. No matter how dire your circumstances may seem, don't give up. Don't allow the enemy to sell you the lie that there is no hope.

The Bible tells us that "against all hope, Abraham in

hope believed" (Rom. 4:18 NIV). In the natural, Abraham's situation was hopeless. His wife could not bear him any children even when she was younger. And now that she was past the natural childbearing age, it was even more impossible. But even when there was no reason to hope, Abraham kept hoping, believing God's promise that he would become a father of many nations. Today we know that God fulfilled His promise as Sarah gave birth to Isaac (see Gen. 21:1–2). The Bible also calls all of us who believe in Christ "sons of Abraham" (see Gal. 3:7).

Do you want to know how you can get Bible hope? Romans 15:4 tells us, "For whatever things were written before were written for our learning, that we through the patience and comfort of the Scriptures might have hope." When you feel yourself spiraling into despair and with no ability to expect good things to ever happen to you, you can get hope from the Scriptures! The Holy Spirit has recorded so many stories that will impart hope to you. Hear the Lord declare to you, "I will. . .make the Valley of Achor a door of hope" (Hosea 2:15 NIV). "Achor" means "trouble."[4] Even when you find yourself in a valley of trouble, God can open a door of hope.

Perhaps life did not turn out the way you expected it to, or a tragedy happened in your life. I can only imagine the pain you must be going through. We live in a fallen world and bad things do happen. But in the midst of your tragedy, can I encourage you to keep hoping? The God of hope is still on the throne. Don't lose heart. The Scriptures promise that you will "see the goodness of the LORD in the land of the living" (Ps. 27:13). Even when tribulations happen in your life, you can glory in them (see Rom. 5:3). The trouble that you are in or the sickness that you might be experiencing did not come from God, but He can take whatever the devil throws at you and make it work together for your good!

CLOSING WORDS

I want to end this book by telling you that your discouragement and depression do not define you. Don't look at yourself and think, *I am an alcoholic/drug addict/cancer patient*, or, *I am depressed/suicidal*. Don't allow the enemy to sell you a pack of lies. You ARE A CHILD OF GOD, and only your heavenly Father has naming rights over you. You are who God says you are, not who the world, the bully in your life, or the enemy says you are. Rachel in the Bible wanted to name her son Ben-Oni, which means "son of my sorrow," because she gave birth to him in pain and sorrow. But Jacob, his father, changed his name to Benjamin, which means "son of my right hand" (Gen. 35:18 NLT).

Don't accept any more mind games from the enemy. You are the son or daughter of Almighty God. You are "a chosen generation, a royal priesthood, a holy nation, His own special people, that you may proclaim the praises of Him who called you out of darkness into His marvelous light" (1 Pet. 2:9)! You are in Christ, seated with Him "at His right hand in the heavenly *places,* far above all principality and power and might and dominion, and every name that is named, not only in this age but also in that which is to come" (Eph. 1:20–21, Eph. 2:6). And "at the name of Jesus every knee should bow, of those in heaven, and of those on earth, and of those under the earth" (Phil. 2:10). Depression has no right to remain in you. Post-traumatic stress disorder has no right to remain in you. Anxiety has no right to remain in you. They have no choice but to bow to the name of Jesus.

Whatever storms you might be faced with right now, and no matter how dire the circumstances might seem, know that the Lord Jesus is with you. *Sar Shalom,* the Prince of Peace, is in your boat, and the wind and waves have no choice but to bow before Him. Do not despair. Do not be afraid—"He who is in you is greater than he who is in the world" (1 John 4:4). With God on your side, you are the majority, and I pray that you will be able to see like Elisha's servant, that those who are with you are more than those who are with your enemies (see 2 Kings 6:16–17).

When you look at the giants in your life, do not be afraid. Because you know your God and all that He has done for you, you can be strong and carry out great exploits (see Dan. 11:32). Because you know your God, you can look at your Goliath and declare, "Who *is* this uncircumcised Philistine, that he should defy the armies of the living God?" (1 Sam. 17:26). Because you know your God, you can look at your giants and see them as bread that will only make you stronger (see Num. 14:9).

I may not know the details of the battle you are fighting, but I know this: The battle is not yours, but God's (see 2 Chron. 20:15). When the battle is His, you will not need to fight. You will only need to "stand still and see the salvation of the LORD, who is with you" (2 Chron. 20:17). It shall be well, my friend. Whatever your giants are, however grim your battle may look, it's not over until His victory is gloriously manifested. Your Lord Jesus will not rest until He has concluded the matter for you (see Ruth 3:18). And right now, I prophesy to you that you shall look for your enemies and not find them. Those who have warred against you shall be as nothing (see Isa. 41:12)!

I am keeping you in prayer, and I am awaiting good

news from you. When your breakthrough comes, be sure to write to my team via JosephPrince.com/testimony. David cut off Goliath's head with the very sword that Goliath had tried to kill him with, and so shall it be for you. There's a saying that goes, "There's no point flogging a dead horse." If you were of no threat to the enemy, the enemy would not have had a reason to attack you. So I believe God has a great plan for your life and that is why the enemy has tried so hard to abort this plan. But you know what? He picked the wrong target. Let your testimony encourage others who are going through similar struggles, and let's make the enemy regret ever trying to lay a finger on you!

GOD'S PROMISES FOR YOU

God loves you and cares about you. He knows there will be days you may feel all alone, days you may feel imprisoned by despair and hopelessness. The Bible is full of promises from God that I believe will encourage you. I have put together the Bible verses I used in this book, as well as other verses that I pray will strengthen you and help you look beyond the challenges you are facing.

"And I have also heard the groaning of the children of Israel whom the Egyptians keep in bondage, and I have remembered My covenant. Therefore say to the children of Israel: 'I *am* the Lord; I will bring you out from under the burdens of the Egyptians, I will rescue you from their bondage, and I will redeem you with an outstretched arm and with great judgments. I will take you as My people, and I will be your God. Then you shall know that I *am* the Lord your God who brings you out from under the burdens of the Egyptians. And I will bring you into the land which I swore to give to Abraham, Isaac, and Jacob; and I will give it to you *as* a heritage: I *am* the Lord.' "

—Exodus 6:5–8

Do not be afraid or discouraged, for the Lord will personally go ahead of you. He will be with you; he will neither fail you nor abandon you.

—**Deuteronomy 31:8 NLT**

You, Lord, are my lamp; the Lord turns my darkness into light.

—**2 Samuel 22:29 NIV**

But You, O Lord, *are* a shield for me,
My glory and the One who lifts up my head.
I cried to the Lord with my voice,
And He heard me from His holy hill.

—**Psalm 3:3–4**

I will both lie down in peace, and sleep;
For You alone, O Lord, make me dwell in safety.

—**Psalm 4:8**

The Lord *is* my shepherd;

I shall not want.

He makes me to lie down in green pastures;

He leads me beside the still waters.

He restores my soul;

He leads me in the paths of righteousness

For His name's sake.

Yea, though I walk through the valley of the
     shadow of death,

I will fear no evil;

For You *are* with me;

Your rod and Your staff, they comfort me.

You prepare a table before me in the presence of
     my enemies;

You anoint my head with oil;

My cup runs over.

Surely goodness and mercy shall follow me

All the days of my life;

And I will dwell in the house of the Lord

Forever.

—Psalm 23:1–6

I would have lost heart, unless I had believed

That I would see the goodness of the LORD

In the land of the living.

Wait on the LORD;

Be of good courage,

And He shall strengthen your heart;

Wait, I say, on the LORD!

—Psalm 27:13–14

The LORD *is* my strength and my shield;

My heart trusted in Him, and I am helped;

Therefore my heart greatly rejoices,

And with my song I will praise Him.

The LORD *is* their strength,

And He *is* the saving refuge of His anointed.

—Psalm 28:7–8

You have turned for me my mourning into dancing;

You have put off my sackcloth and clothed me with

gladness.

—**Psalm 30:11**

As for me, I said in my alarm,

"I am cut off from Your eyes."

Nevertheless You heard the voice of my

supplications (specific requests)

When I cried to You [for help]….

Be strong and let your hearts take courage,

All you who wait for *and* confidently expect

the Lord.

—**Psalm 31:22, 24 AMP**

The Lord hears his people when they call to

him for help.

He rescues them from all their troubles.

The Lord is close to the brokenhearted;

he rescues those whose spirits are crushed.

The righteous person faces many troubles,

but the L ORD comes to the rescue each time.

—Psalm 34:17–19 NLT

The L ORD directs the steps of the godly.

He delights in every detail of their lives.

Though they stumble, they will never fall,

for the L ORD holds them by the hand.

—Psalm 37:23–24 NLT

He also brought me up out of a horrible pit,

Out of the miry clay,

And set my feet upon a rock,

And established my steps.

He has put a new song in my mouth.

—Psalm 40:2–3

God *is* our refuge and strength,

A very present help in trouble.

—Psalm 46:1

He who dwells in the secret place of the Most High

Shall abide under the shadow of the Almighty.

I will say of the Lord, "*He is* my refuge and

my fortress;

My God, in Him I will trust."

—Psalm 91:1–2

Give thanks to the Lord, for he is good!

His faithful love endures forever.

—Psalm 118:29 NLT

Your faithfulness *endures* to all generations;

You established the earth, and it abides.

—Psalm 119:90

I will lift up my eyes to the hills—

From whence comes my help?

My help *comes* from the Lord,

Who made heaven and earth.

He will not allow your foot to be moved;

He who keeps you will not slumber.

Behold, He who keeps Israel

Shall neither slumber nor sleep.

The Lord *is* your keeper;

The Lord *is* your shade at your right hand.

The sun shall not strike you by day,

Nor the moon by night.

The Lord shall preserve you from all evil;

He shall preserve your soul.

The Lord shall preserve your going out and your
coming in

From this time forth, and even forevermore.

—Psalm 121:1–8

It is vain for you to rise early,

To retire late,

To eat the bread of anxious labors—

For He gives [blessings] to His beloved *even in*

his sleep.

—Psalm 127:2 AMP

The LORD upholds all who fall and lifts up all who

are bowed down.

—Psalm 145:14 NIV

He heals the brokenhearted

And binds up their wounds.

—Psalm 147:3

For they [God's Word] *are* life to those who find them,

And health to all their flesh.

—Proverbs 4:22

Two people are better off than one, for they can help each other succeed. If one person falls, the other can reach out and help. But someone who falls alone is in real trouble.

—Ecclesiastes 4:9–10 NLT

And it shall come to pass in that day, *that* his burden shall be taken away from off thy shoulder, and his yoke from off thy neck, and the yoke shall be destroyed because of the anointing.

—Isaiah 10:27 KJV

You will keep in perfect peace
all who trust in you,
all whose thoughts are fixed on you!

—Isaiah 26:3 NLT

He gives power to the weak,

And to *those who have* no might He
increases strength.

Even the youths shall faint and be weary,

And the young men shall utterly fall,

But those who wait on the LORD

Shall renew *their* strength;

They shall mount up with wings like eagles,

They shall run and not be weary,

They shall walk and not faint.

—Isaiah 40:29–31

"Don't be afraid, for I am with you.

Don't be discouraged, for I am your God.

I will strengthen you and help you.

I will hold you up with my victorious right hand."

—Isaiah 41:10 NLT

"You will look in vain
for those who tried to conquer you.
Those who attack you
will come to nothing."

—Isaiah 41:12 NLT

He is despised and rejected by men,
A Man of sorrows and acquainted with grief.
And we hid, as it were, *our* faces from Him;
He was despised, and we did not esteem Him.
Surely He has borne our griefs
And carried our sorrows;
Yet we esteemed Him stricken,
Smitten by God, and afflicted.
But He *was* wounded for our transgressions,
He was bruised for our iniquities;
The chastisement for our peace was upon Him,
And by His stripes we are healed.

—Isaiah 53:3–5

"No weapon formed against you shall prosper,

And every tongue *which* rises against you

   in judgment

You shall condemn.

This *is* the heritage of the servants of the LORD,

And their righteousness *is* from Me,"

Says the LORD.

—Isaiah 54:17

"To console those who mourn in Zion,

To give them beauty for ashes,

The oil of joy for mourning,

The garment of praise for the spirit of heaviness;

That they may be called trees of righteousness,

The planting of the LORD, that He may be glorified."

—Isaiah 61:3

Instead of your shame *you shall have* double *honor*,

And *instead of* confusion they shall rejoice in

their portion.

Therefore in their land they shall possess double;

Everlasting joy shall be theirs.

—Isaiah 61:7

"Blessed *is* the man who trusts in the Lord,

And whose hope is the Lord.

For he shall be like a tree planted by the waters,

Which spreads out its roots by the river,

And will not fear when heat comes;

But its leaf will be green,

And will not be anxious in the year of drought,

Nor will cease from yielding fruit."

—Jeremiah 17:7–8

"I will set up shepherds over them who will feed them; and they shall fear no more, nor be dismayed, nor shall they be lacking," says the Lord.

—Jeremiah 23:4

For I know the thoughts that I think toward you, says the Lord, thoughts of peace and not of evil, to give you a future and a hope.

—Jeremiah 29:11

"There I will give her back her vineyards, and will make the Valley of Achor a door of hope."

—Hosea 2:15 NIV

For the Lord your God is living among you.
He is a mighty savior.
He will take delight in you with gladness.
With his love, he will calm all your fears.
He will rejoice over you with joyful songs.

—Zephaniah 3:17 NLT

"Come back to the place of safety,

all you prisoners who still have hope!

I promise this very day

that I will repay two blessings for each of

 your troubles."

—Zechariah 9:12 NLT

"Therefore I say to you, do not worry about your
life, what you will eat or what you will drink; nor
about your body, what you will put on. Is not
life more than food and the body more than cloth-
ing? Look at the birds of the air, for they neither
sow nor reap nor gather into barns; yet your
heavenly Father feeds them. Are you not of more
value than they?"

—Matthew 6:25–26

"Come to Me, all *you* who labor and are heavy laden, and I will give you rest."

—Matthew 11:28

"But these are the ones sown on good ground, those who hear the word, accept *it,* and bear fruit: some thirtyfold, some sixty, and some a hundred."

—Mark 4:20

"The thief does not come except to steal, and to kill, and to destroy. I have come that they may have life, and that they may have *it* more abundantly."

—John 10:10

"Here on earth you will have many trials and sorrows. But take heart, because I have overcome the world."

—John 16:33 NLT

We can rejoice, too, when we run into problems
and trials, for we know that they help us develop
endurance. And endurance develops strength of
character, and character strengthens our confident
hope of salvation. And this hope will not lead to
disappointment.

—Romans 5:3–5 NLT

What then shall we say to these things? If God *is* for
us, who *can be* against us?

—Romans 8:31

May the God of hope fill you with all joy and peace
as you trust in him, so that you may overflow with
hope by the power of the Holy Spirit.

—Romans 15:13 NIV

But of Him you are in Christ Jesus, who became for us wisdom from God—and righteousness and sanctification and redemption.

—1 Corinthians 1:30

No temptation has overtaken you except such as is common to man; but God *is* faithful, who will not allow you to be tempted beyond what you are able, but with the temptation will also make the way of escape, that you may be able to bear *it.*

—1 Corinthians 10:13

Praise be to the God and Father of our Lord Jesus Christ, the Father of compassion and the God of all comfort, who comforts us in all our troubles, so that we can comfort those in any trouble with the comfort we ourselves receive from God.

—2 Corinthians 1:3–4 NIV

Now the Lord is the Spirit; and where the Spirit of the Lord *is*, there *is* liberty.

—2 Corinthians 3:17

But we all, with unveiled face, beholding as in a mirror the glory of the Lord, are being transformed into the same image from glory to glory, just as by the Spirit of the Lord.

—2 Corinthians 3:18

Therefore, if anyone *is* in Christ, *he is* a new creation; old things have passed away; behold, all things have become new.

—2 Corinthians 5:17

For He made Him who knew no sin *to be* sin for us, that we might become the righteousness of God in Him.

—2 Corinthians 5:21

For you know the grace of our Lord Jesus Christ, that though He was rich, yet for your sakes He became poor, that you through His poverty might become rich.

—**2 Corinthians 8:9**

Christ has redeemed us from the curse of the law, having become a curse for us (for it is written, "Cursed *is* everyone who hangs on a tree"), that the blessing of Abraham might come upon the Gentiles in Christ Jesus, that we might receive the promise of the Spirit through faith.

—**Galatians 3:13–14**

Blessed *be* the God and Father of our Lord Jesus Christ, who has blessed us with every spiritual blessing in the heavenly *places* in Christ.

—**Ephesians 1:3**

In Him we have redemption through His blood, the forgiveness of sins, according to the riches of His grace.

—Ephesians 1:7

Now to Him who is able to do exceedingly abundantly above all that we ask or think, according to the power that works in us.

—Ephesians 3:20

Stand therefore, having girded your waist with truth, having put on the breastplate of righteousness, and having shod your feet with the preparation of the gospel of peace; above all, taking the shield of faith with which you will be able to quench all the fiery darts of the wicked one. And take the helmet of salvation, and the sword of the Spirit, which is the word of God.

—Ephesians 6:14–17

Be anxious for nothing, but in everything by prayer and supplication, with thanksgiving, let your requests be made known to God; and the peace of God, which surpasses all understanding, will guard your hearts and minds through Christ Jesus.

—Philippians 4:6–7

Finally, brethren, whatever things are true, whatever things *are* noble, whatever things *are* just, whatever things *are* pure, whatever things *are* lovely, whatever things *are* of good report, if *there is* any virtue and if *there is* anything praiseworthy—meditate on these things.

—Philippians 4:8

And my God shall supply all your need according to His riches in glory by Christ Jesus.

—Philippians 4:19

So let us come boldly to the throne of our gracious God. There we will receive his mercy, and we will find grace to help us when we need it most.

—**Hebrews 4:16** NLT

He has said, "I WILL NEVER [under any circumstances] DESERT YOU [nor give you up nor leave you without support, nor will I in any degree leave you helpless], NOR WILL I FORSAKE *or* LET YOU DOWN *or* RELAX MY HOLD ON YOU [assuredly not]!"

—**Hebrews 13:5** AMP

But you *are* a chosen generation, a royal priesthood, a holy nation, His own special people, that you may proclaim the praises of Him who called you out of darkness into His marvelous light.

—**1 Peter 2:9**

Therefore humble yourselves under the mighty hand of God, that He may exalt you in due time, casting all your care upon Him, for He cares for you. Be sober, be vigilant; because your adversary the devil walks about like a roaring lion, seeking whom he may devour. Resist him, steadfast in the faith, knowing that the same sufferings are experienced by your brotherhood in the world.

—1 Peter 5:6–9

Casting all your cares [all your anxieties, all your worries, and all your concerns, once and for all] on Him, for He cares about you [with deepest affection, and watches over you very carefully].

—1 Peter 5:7 AMP

Love has been perfected among us in this: that we may have boldness in the day of judgment; because as He is, so are we in this world.

—1 John 4:17

NOTES

Chapter One: You Are Not Alone

1. Ducharme, Jamie. "A Disturbing Trend on the Rise." *Time*, June 18, 2018. http://time.com/5304227/suicide-on-the-rise/.

2. OT: 3444, Joseph Henry Thayer, Francis Brown, Samuel Rolles Driver, and Charles Augustus Briggs, *The Online Bible Thayer's Greek Lexicon and Brown Driver & Briggs Hebrew Lexicon*. Copyright © 1993, Woodside Bible Fellowship, Ontario, Canada. Licensed from the Institute for Creation Research.

Chapter Three: Don't Let the Enemy Mess with You

1. Shrier, Cahleen. "The Science of the Crucifixion," *APU Life* (Spring 2002). https://www.apu.edu/articles/15657/.

2. OT: 2781, James Strong, *Biblesoft's New Exhaustive Strong's Numbers and Concordance with Expanded Greek-Hebrew Dictionary*. Copyright © 1994, 2003, 2006 Biblesoft, Inc. and International Bible Translators, Inc.

3. "Bullying and Depression." *Bullying Statistics: Anti-Bullying Help, Facts, and More*. Retrieved August 1, 2018, from http://www.bullyingstatistics.org/content/bullying-and-depression.html.

4. Bevilacqua M., Fanti G., D'Arienzo M. "The Causes of Jesus' Death in the Light of the Holy Bible and the Turin Shroud." *Open Journal of Trauma* 1(2) (April 11, 2017): 037-046. DOI: http://dx.doi.org/10.17352/ojt.000009.

Chapter Four: Practical Keys to Break Free

1. Mercola, Joseph. "How Sunlight Affects Your Mental Health." Retrieved August 2, 2018, from https://articles.mercola.com/sites/articles/archive/2016/12/01/sunlight-depression.aspx.

2. OT: 5027, James Strong, *Biblesoft's New Exhaustive Strong's Numbers and Concordance with Expanded Greek-Hebrew Dictionary*. Copyright © 1994, 2003, 2006 Biblesoft, Inc. and International Bible Translators, Inc.

3. NT: 1680, William Edwy Vine, *Vine's Expository Dictionary of Biblical Words*. Copyright © 1985, Thomas Nelson Publishers.

4. OT: 5911, Joseph Henry Thayer, Francis Brown, Samuel Rolles Driver, and Charles Augustus Briggs, *The Online Bible Thayer's Greek Lexicon and Brown Driver & Briggs Hebrew Lexicon*. Copyright © 1993, Woodside Bible Fellowship, Ontario, Canada. Licensed from the Institute for Creation Research.

EXTRA RESOURCES

To hear Joseph Prince preach on the biblical principles
and truths shared in each chapter of this book,
please check out the following audio messages at
JosephPrince.com/mindgames:

Chapter One

Win over Discouragement, Depression and Burnout

Peace Keeps What Grace Gives

Receive Restoration as You Walk with Jesus

Just a Groan Will Reach the Throne

How to Pray When You Have No Prayer

Chapter Two

The Power of Right Believing

What "Spiritual Blessings" and "Redemption" Really Mean

Five Words to Live By—The Battle Is the Lord's

Your Inheritance—All Things Work Together for Good

Chapter Three

Why the Finished Work Begins in Your Mind

See the Father's Love for You (Part 2)

A Love Beyond Time—The Bride of Christ

The Cross—Your Redemption from Shame and Reproach

Got a Weakness? God Can Use You!

Double Honor for Your Shame

Chapter Four

Why You Can Hope against All Hope

Why the Finished Work Begins in Your Mind

Look at the Bronze Serpent—God's Provision for Your Every Need

Under Attack? Put On the Armor of God!

The Power of Right Believing

Learn to See What God Sees

Never Alone, Always Cared For

SALVATION PRAYER

If you would like to receive all that Jesus has done for you and make Him your Lord and Savior, please pray this prayer:

Lord Jesus, thank You for loving me and dying for me on the cross. Your precious blood washes me clean of every sin. You are my Lord and my Savior, now and forever. I believe You rose from the dead and that You are alive today. Because of Your finished work, I am now a beloved child of God and heaven is my home. Thank You for giving me eternal life and filling my heart with Your peace and joy. Amen.

WE WOULD LIKE TO HEAR FROM YOU

If you have prayed the salvation prayer or if you have a testimony to share after reading this book, please send it to us via JosephPrince.com/testimony.

SPECIAL APPRECIATION

Special thanks and appreciation to all who have sent in their testimonies and praise reports to us. Kindly note that all testimonies are received in good faith and edited only for brevity and fluency. Names have been changed to protect the writers' privacy.

STAY CONNECTED
WITH JOSEPH

Connect with Joseph through these social media channels and receive daily inspirational teachings:

Facebook.com/JosephPrince

Twitter.com/JosephPrince

Youtube.com/JosephPrinceOnline

Instagram: @JosephPrince

FREE DAILY E-MAIL
DEVOTIONAL

Sign up for Joseph's free daily email devotional at JosephPrince.com/meditate and receive bite-size inspirations to help you grow in grace.

BOOKS BY
JOSEPH PRINCE

LIVE THE LET-GO LIFE

Live the Let-Go Life is the go-to resource for anyone who wants to find freedom from the stress and anxieties of modern living. Instead of letting stress and all its negative effects rule your life, discover how you can cast all your cares to the One who cares about you like no other, and experience His practical supply for every need. You'll find simple yet powerful truths and tools to help you get rid of worry and anxiety and experience greater health and well-being. Learn how you can tune in to God's peace, walk daily in His unforced rhythm of grace, and find yourself living healthier, happier, and having time for the important things in life!

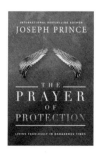

THE PRAYER OF PROTECTION

We live in dangerous times. A time in which terrorist activities, pandemics, and natural calamities are on the rise. But there is good news. God has given us a powerful prayer of protection—Psalm 91—through which we and our families can find safety and deliverance from every snare of the enemy. In *The Prayer of Protection*, discover a God of love and His impenetrable shield of protection that covers everything that concerns you, and start living fearlessly in these dangerous times!

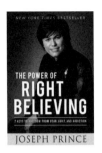

THE POWER OF RIGHT BELIEVING

Experience transformation, breakthroughs, and freedom today through the power of right believing! This book offers seven practical and powerful keys that will help you find freedom from all fears, guilt, and addictions. See these keys come alive in the many precious testimonies you will read from people around the world who have experienced breakthroughs and liberty from all kinds of bondages. Win the battle for your mind through understanding the powerful truths of God's Word and begin a journey of victorious living and unshakable confidence in God's love for you!

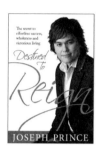

DESTINED TO REIGN

This pivotal and quintessential book on the grace of God will change your life forever! Join Joseph Prince as he unlocks foundational truths to understanding God's grace and how it alone sets you free to experience victory over every adversity, lack, and destructive habit that is limiting you today. Be uplifted and refreshed as you discover how reigning in life is all about Jesus and what He has already done for you. Start experiencing the success, wholeness, and victory that you were destined to enjoy!

ABOUT THE AUTHOR

JOSEPH PRINCE is a leading voice in proclaiming the gospel of grace to a whole new generation of believers and leaders. He is the senior pastor of New Creation Church in Singapore, a vibrant and dynamic church with a congregation of more than 30,000 attendees. He separately heads Joseph Prince Ministries, one of the fastest-growing television broadcast ministries in the world today, reaching millions with the gospel of grace. Joseph is also the best-selling author of *The Power of Right Believing* and *Destined to Reign*, and a highly sought-after conference speaker. For more information about his other inspiring resources, visit www.JosephPrince.com.